Unicorn

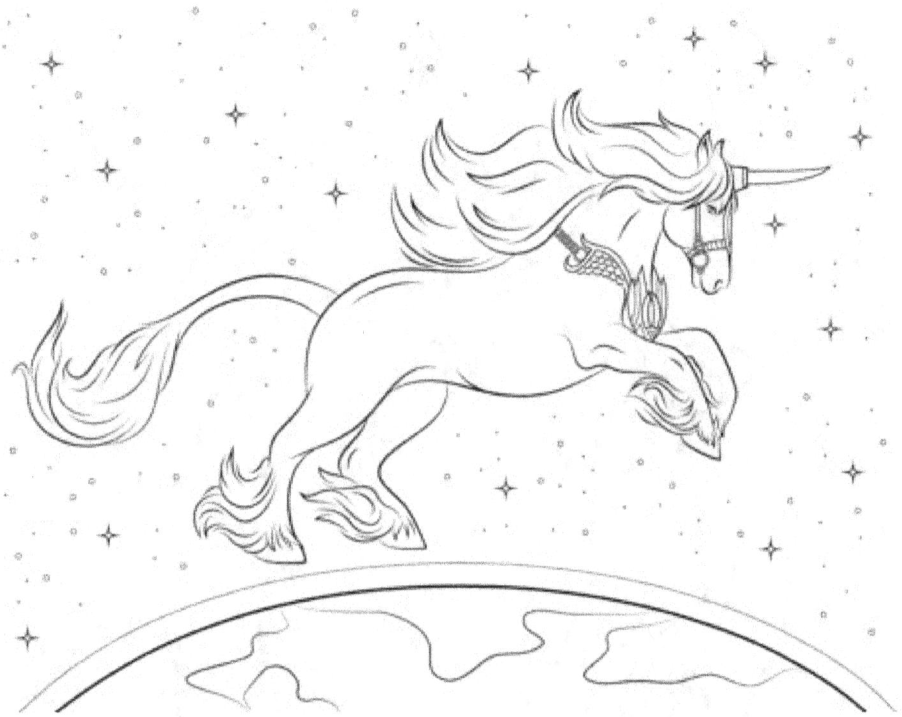

Drawing/Paint book

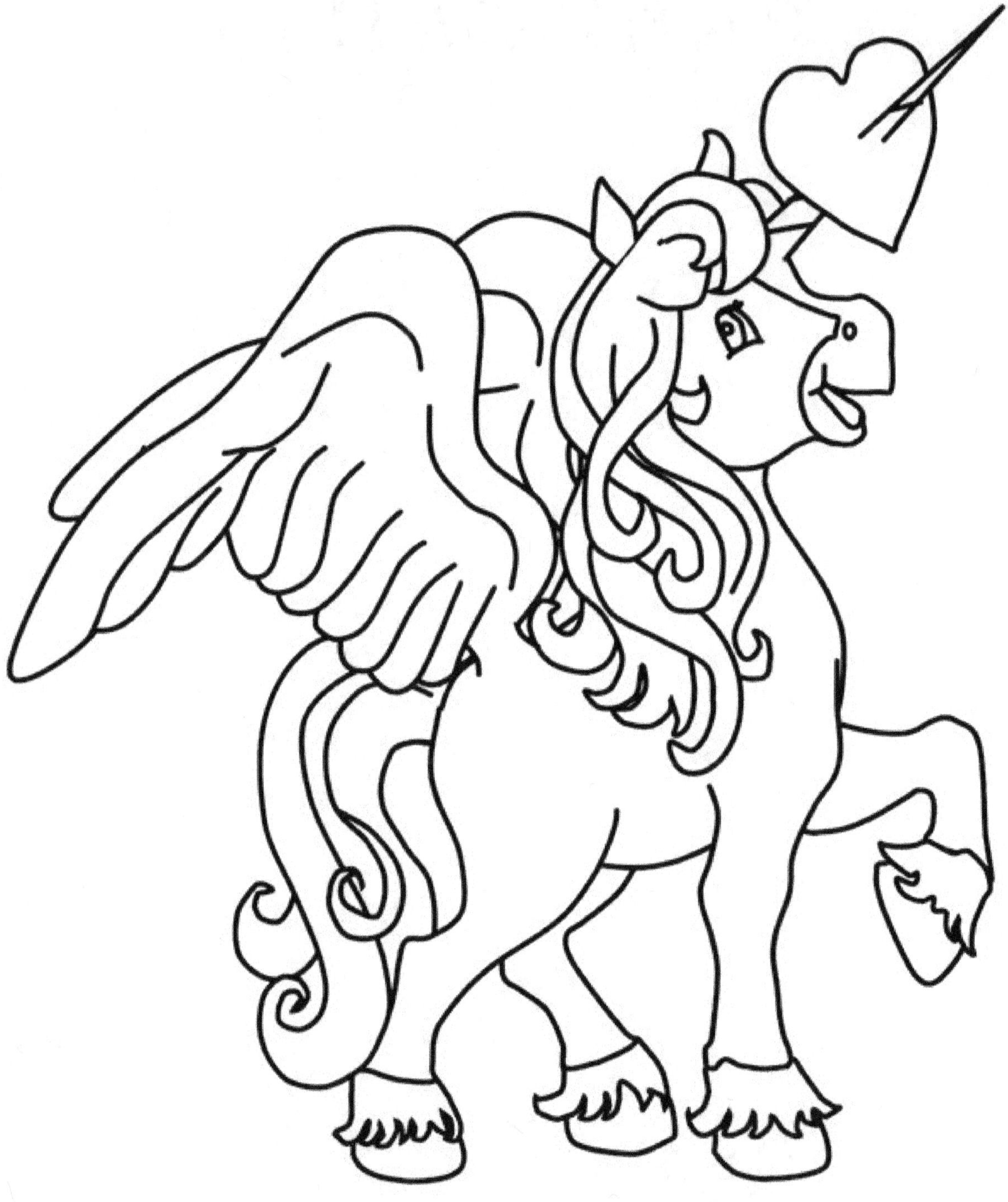

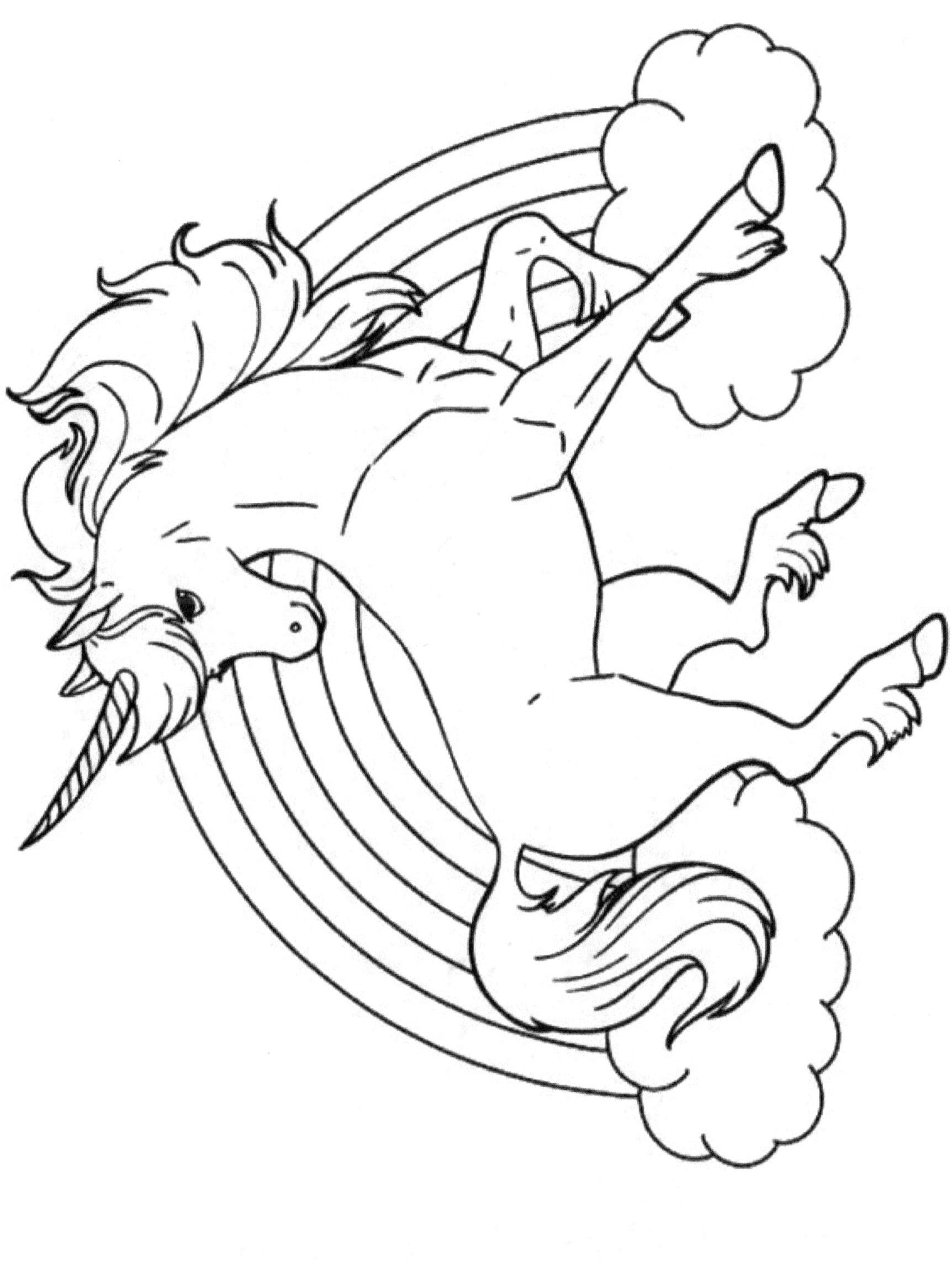

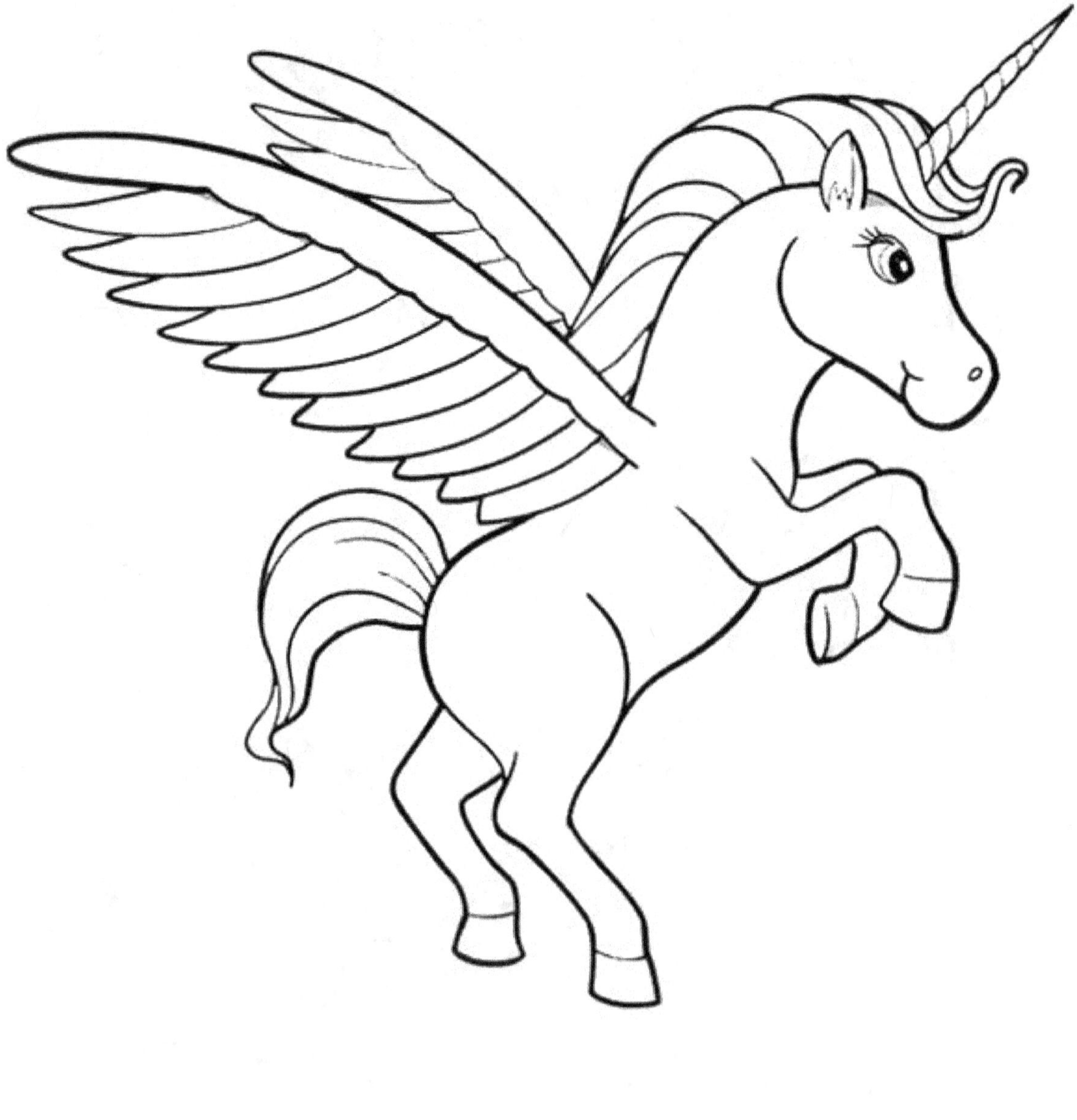

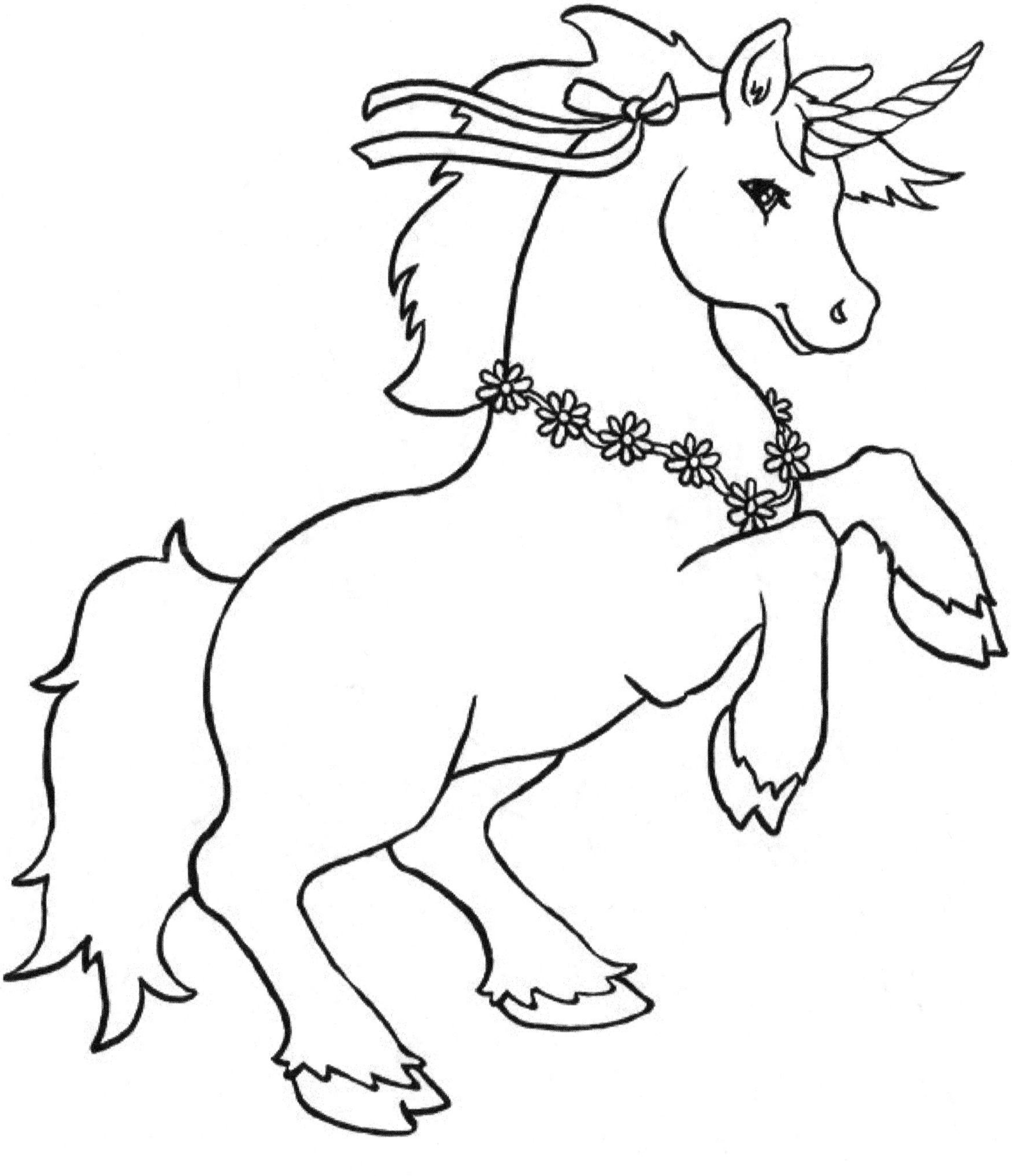

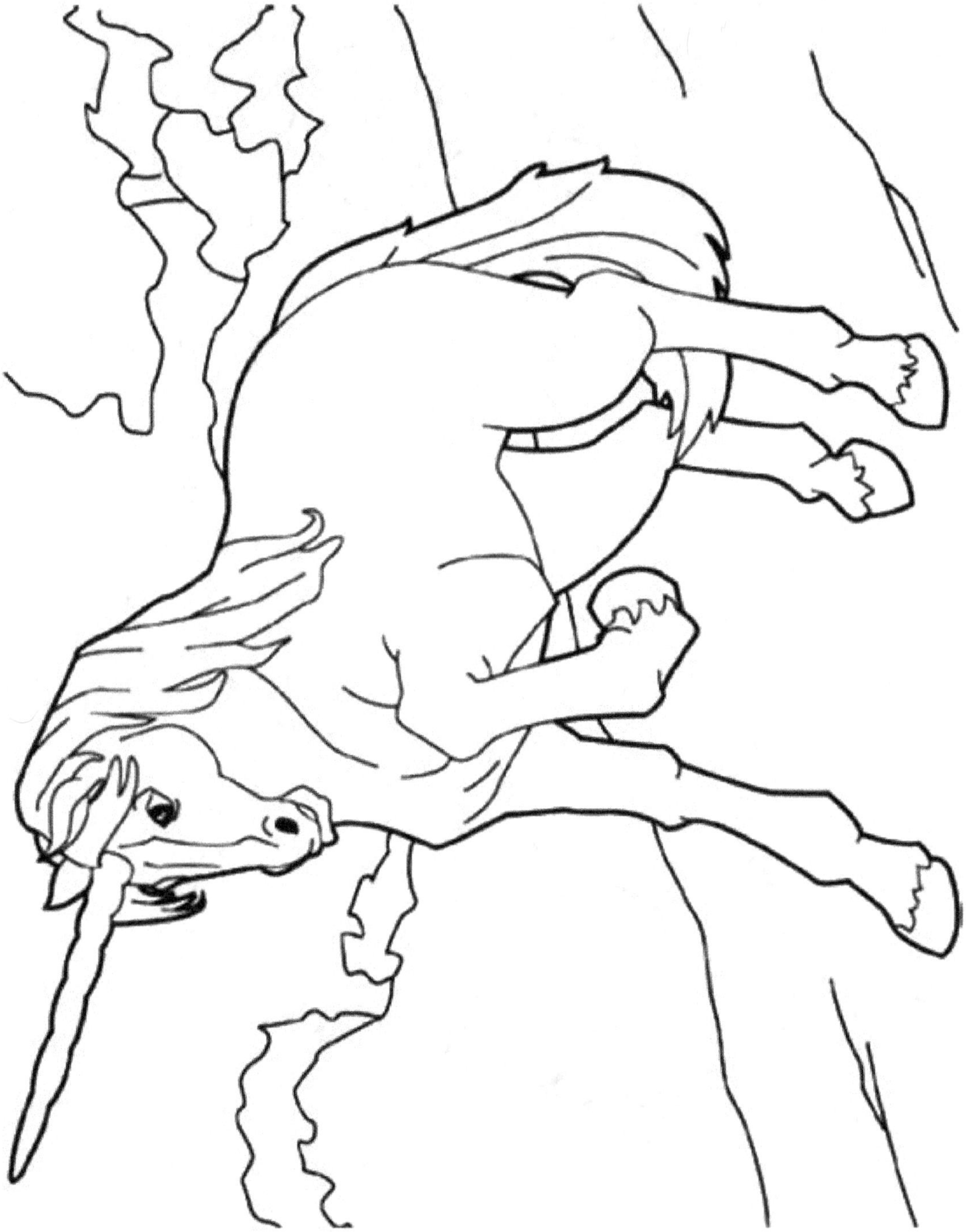

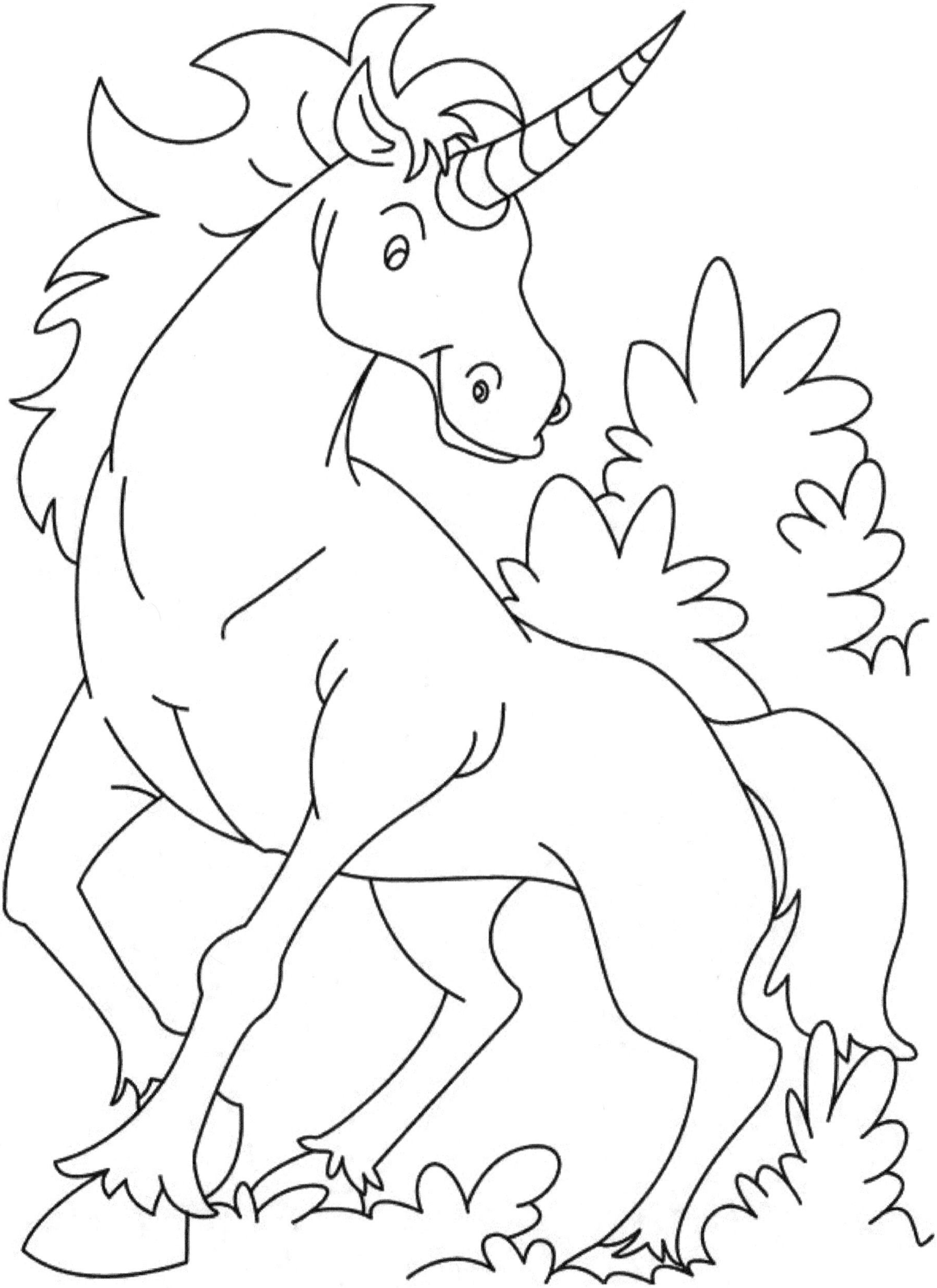

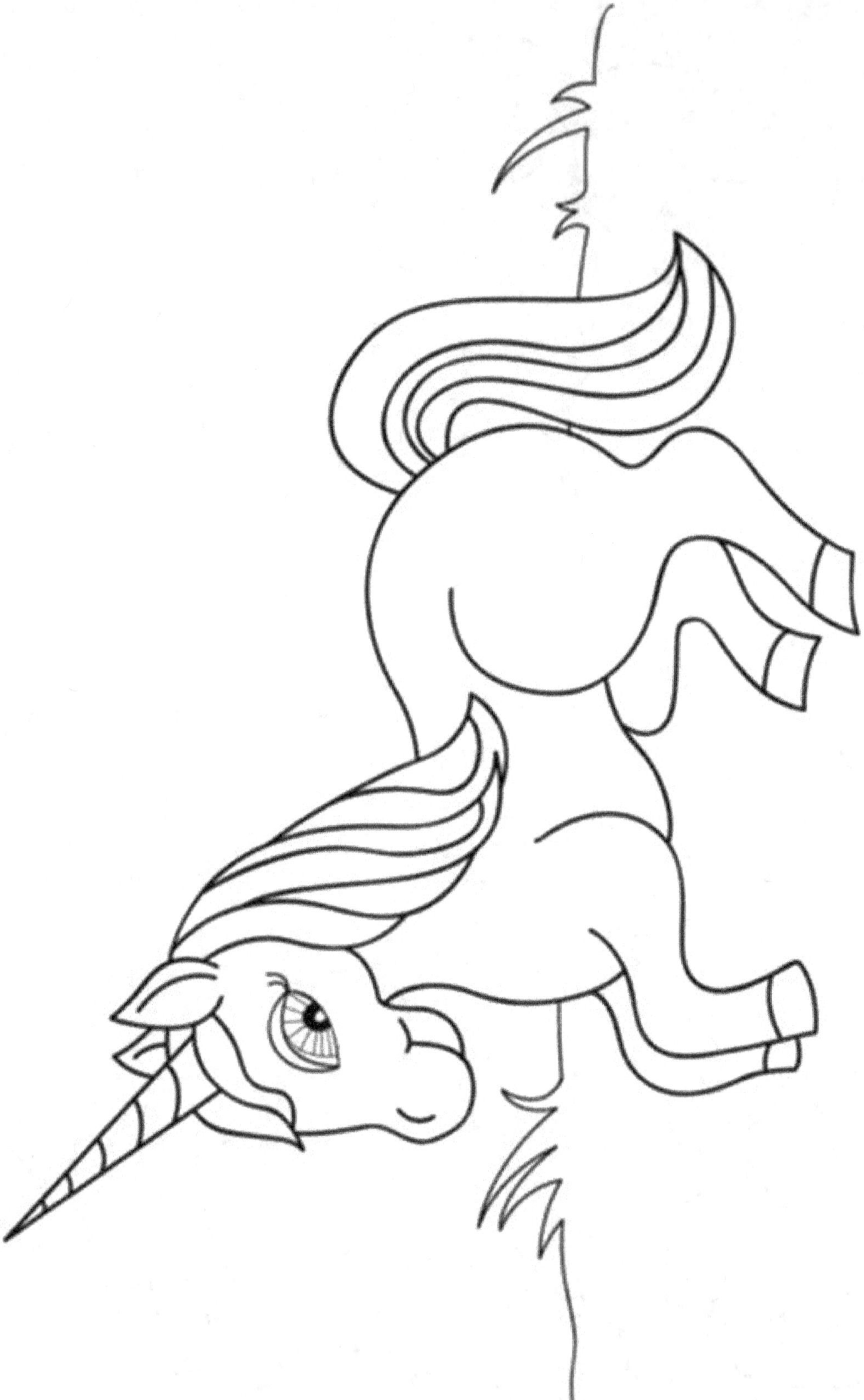

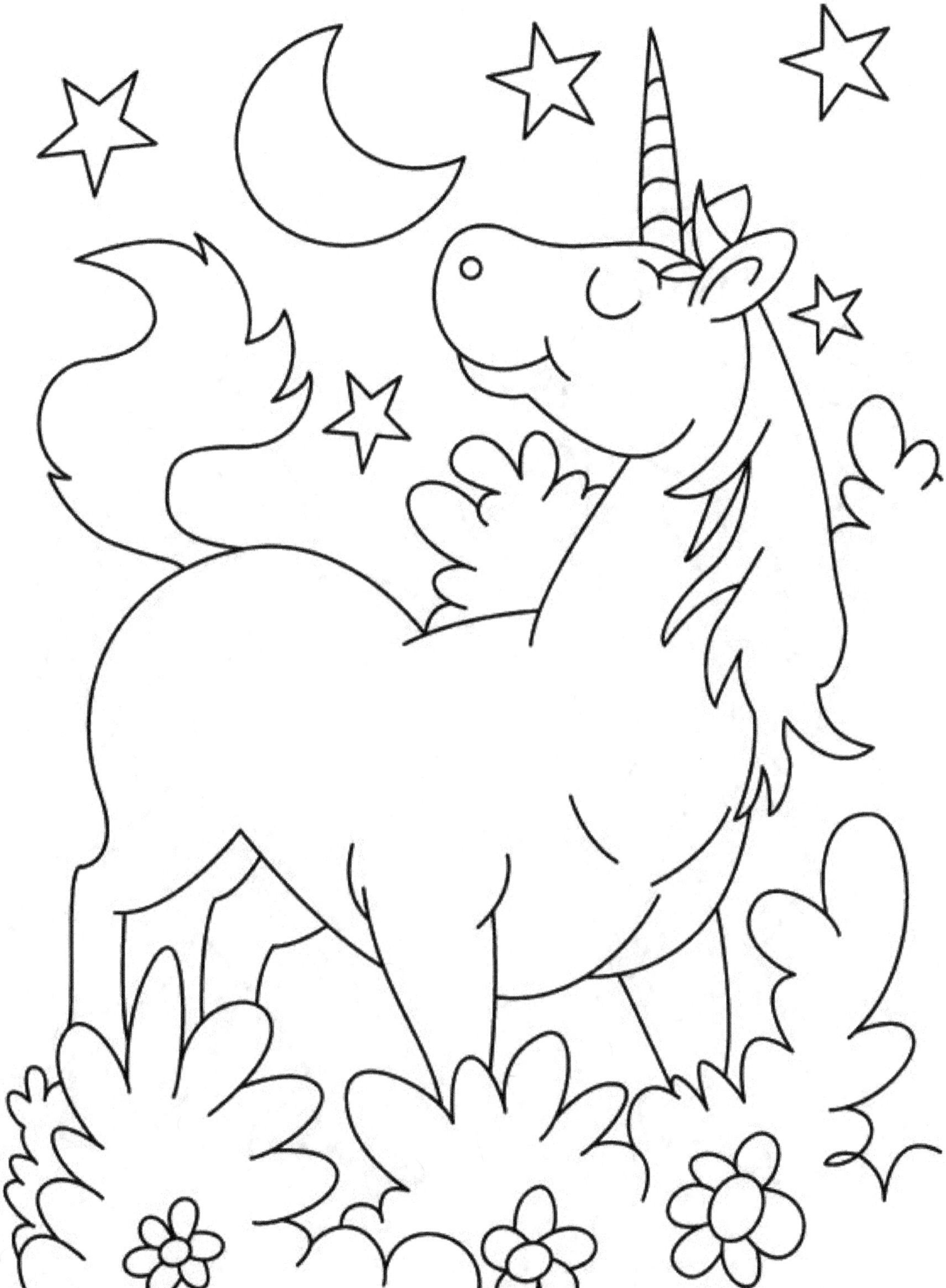

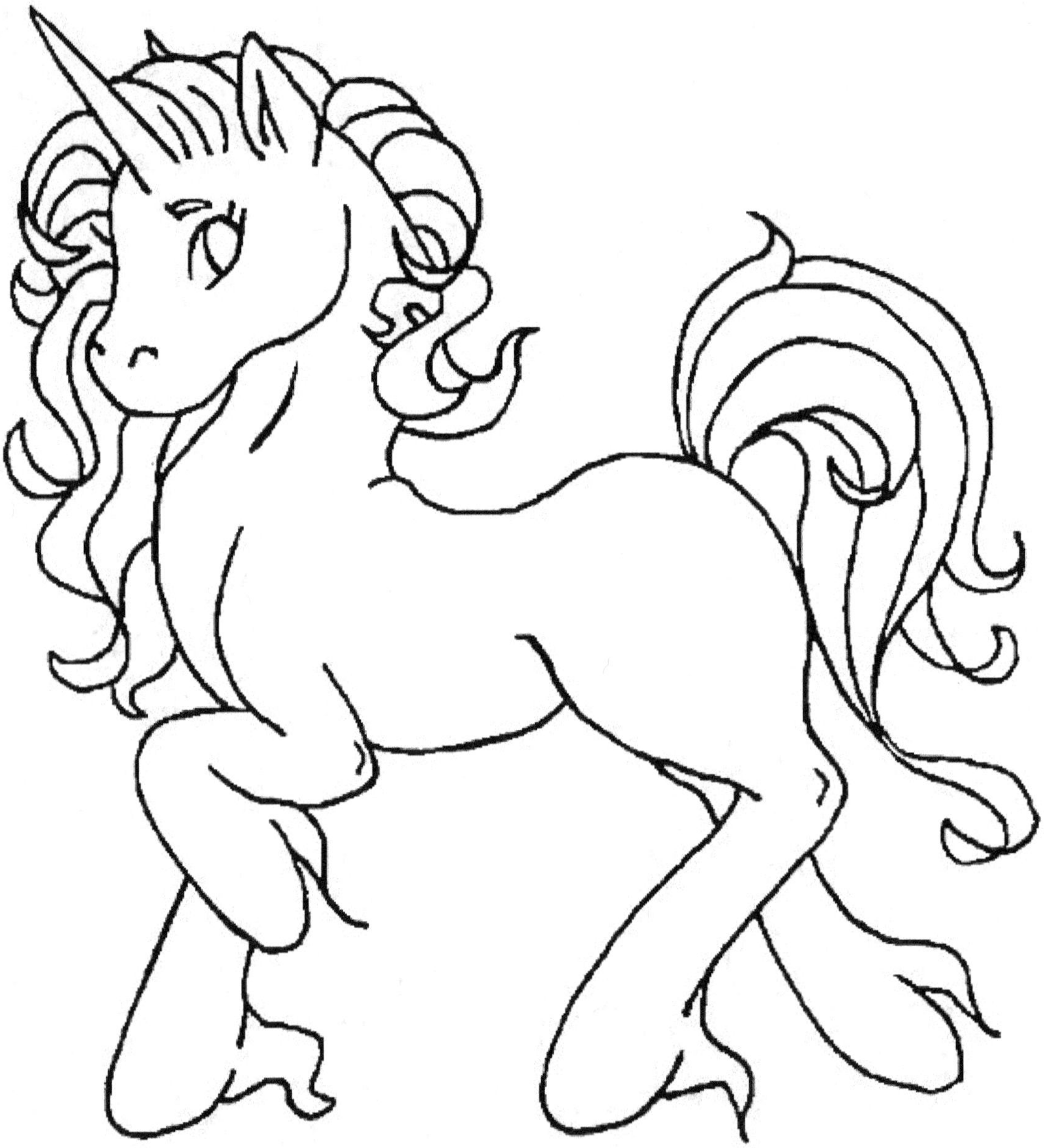

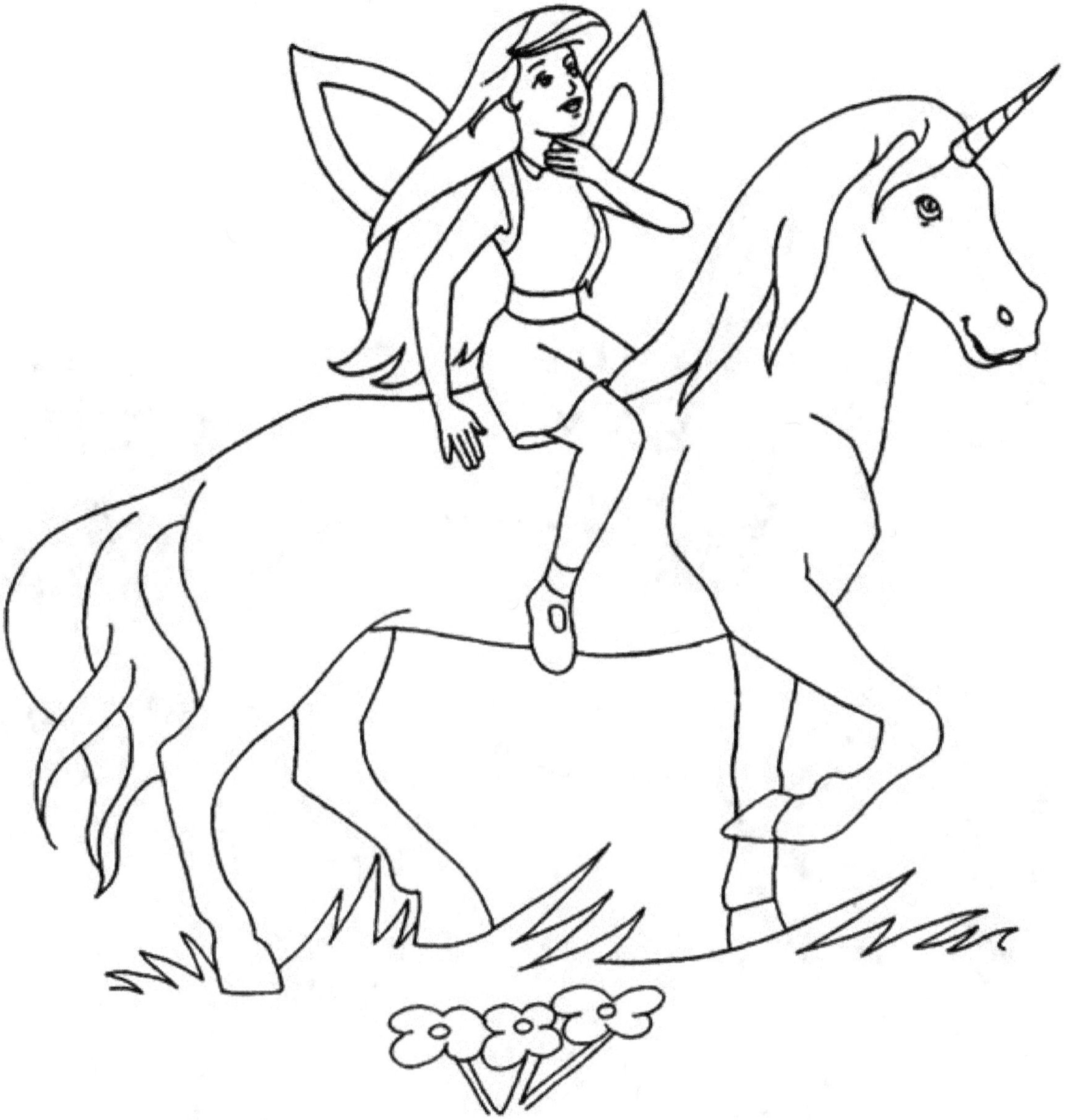

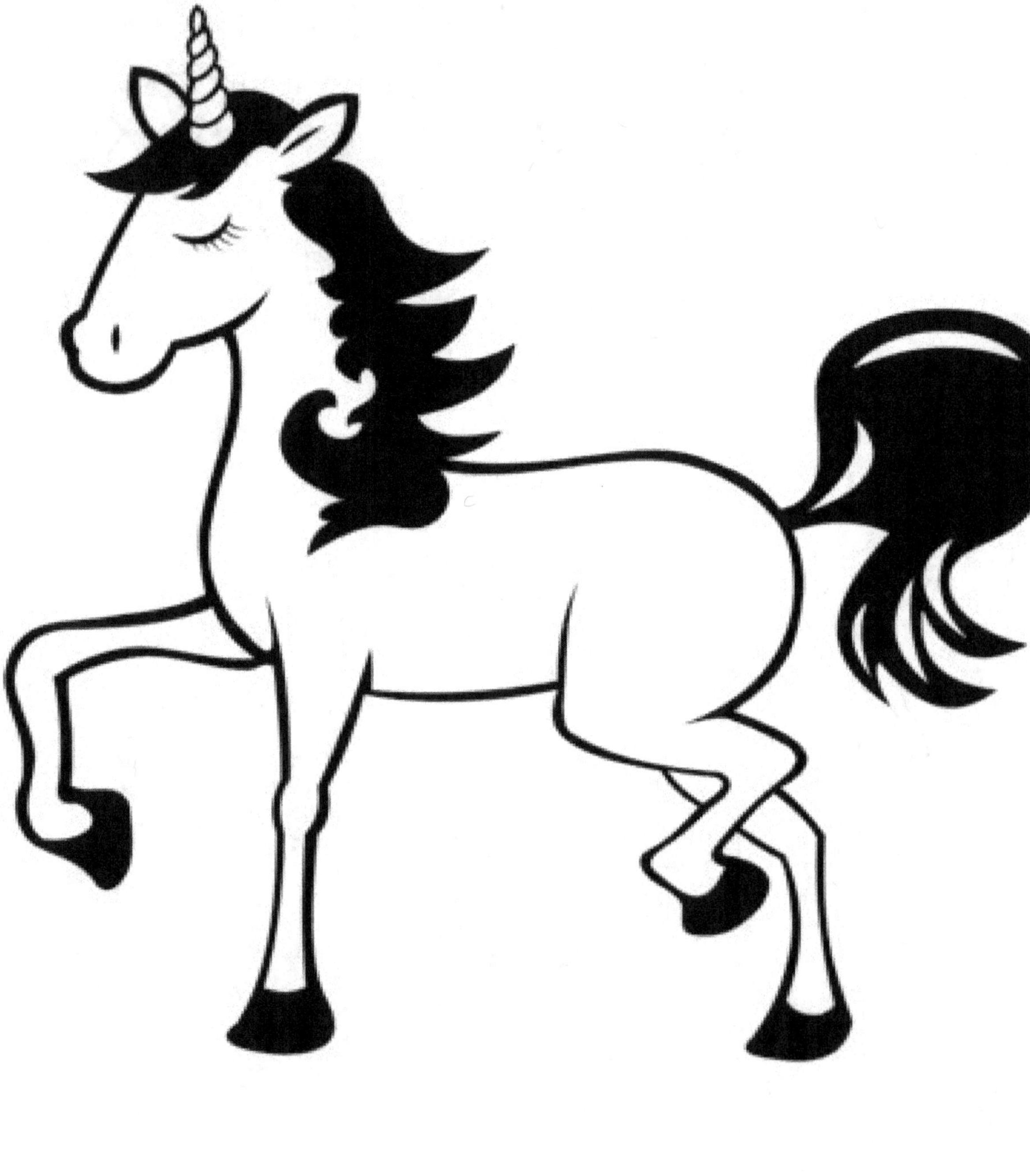

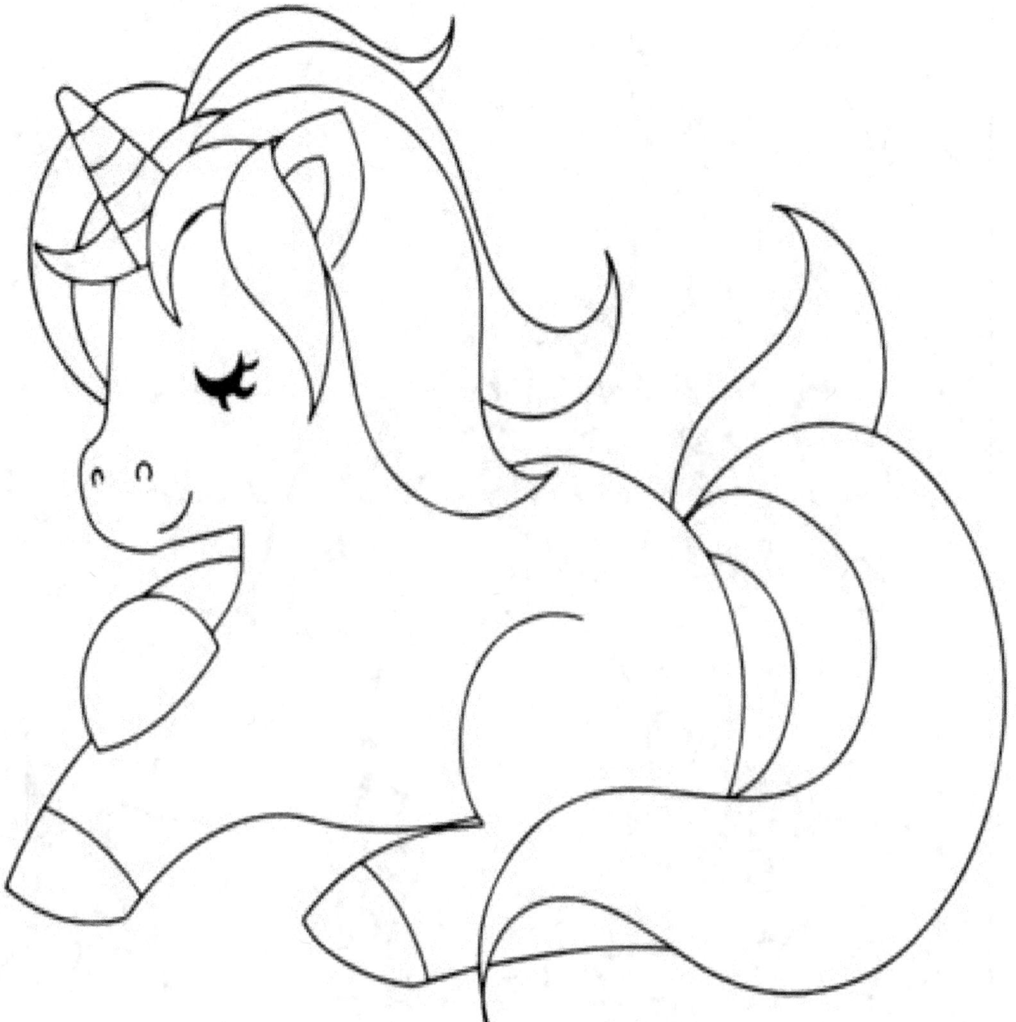

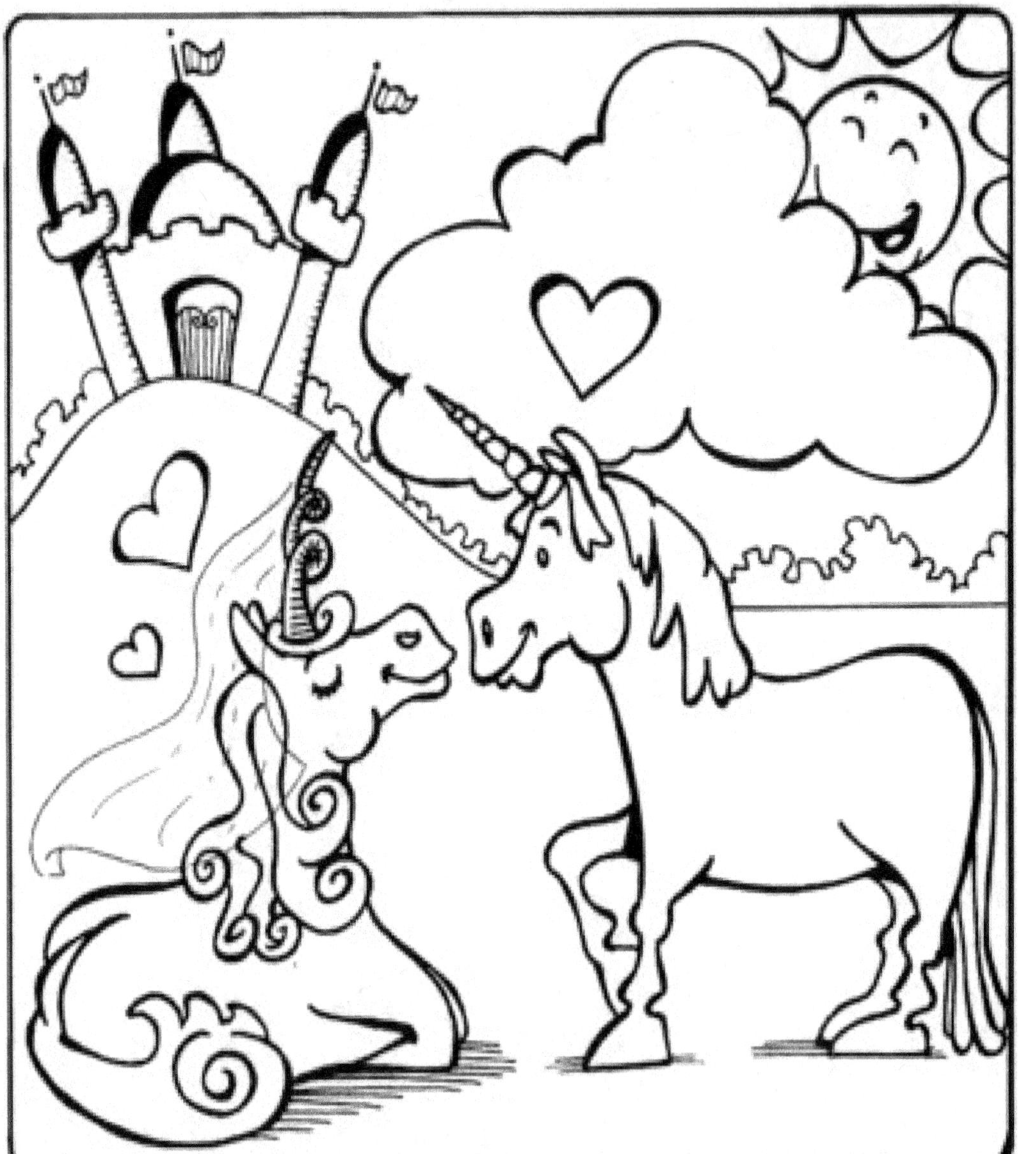

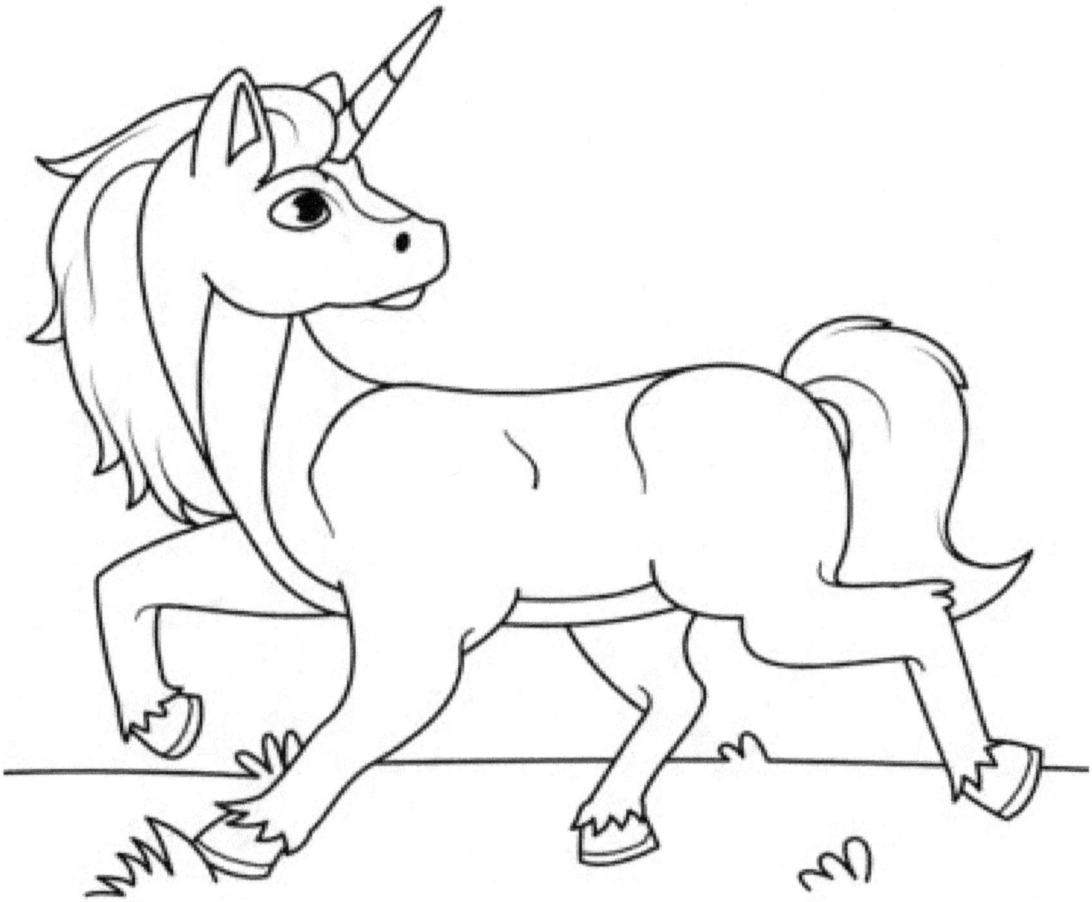

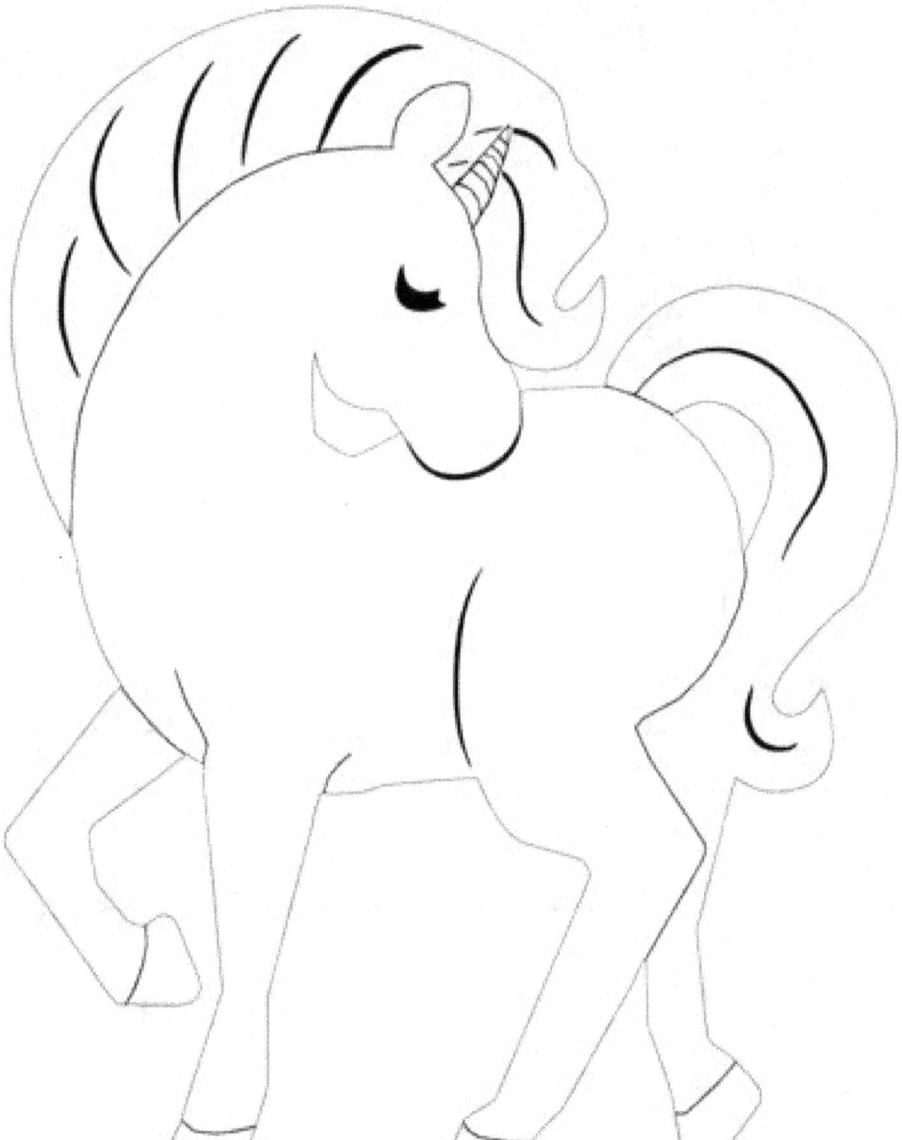

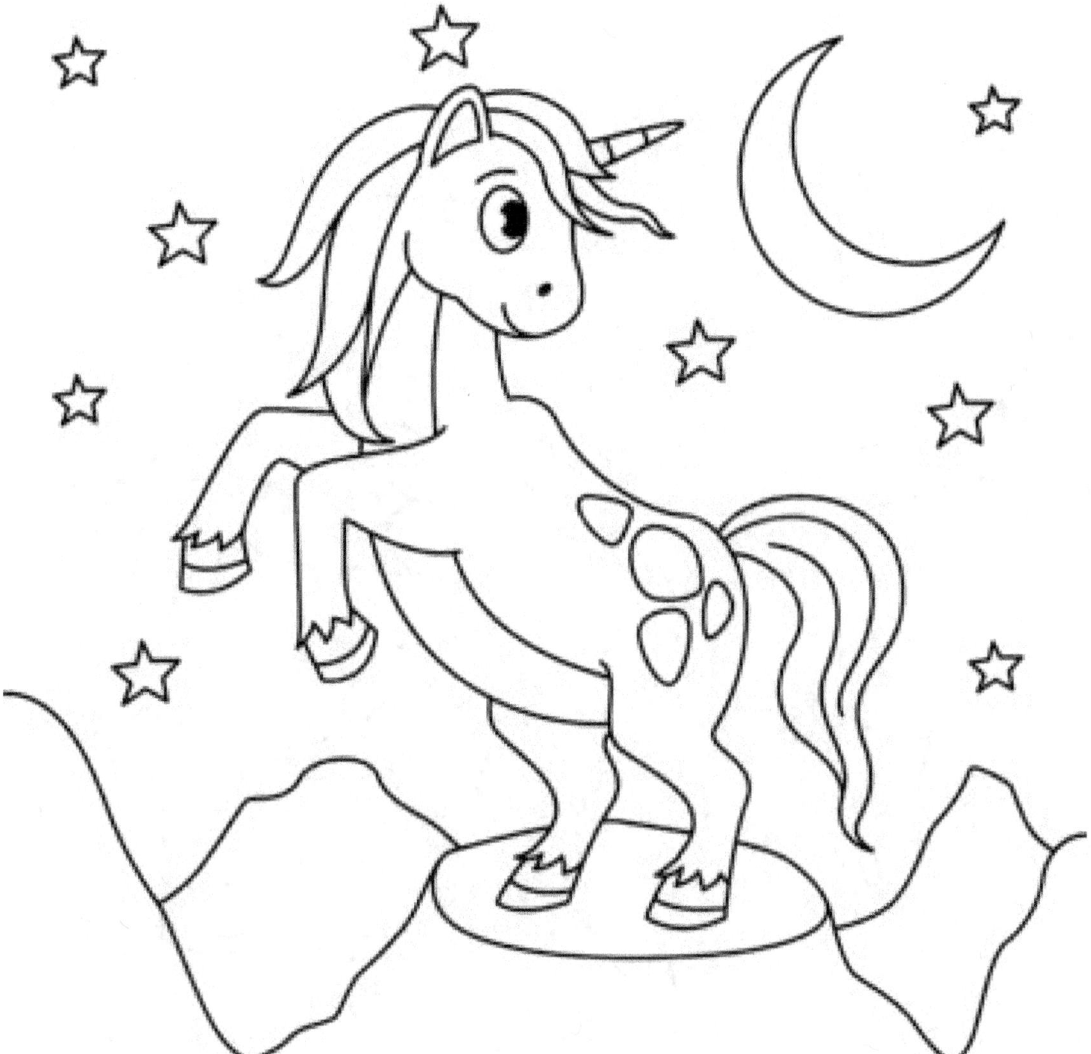

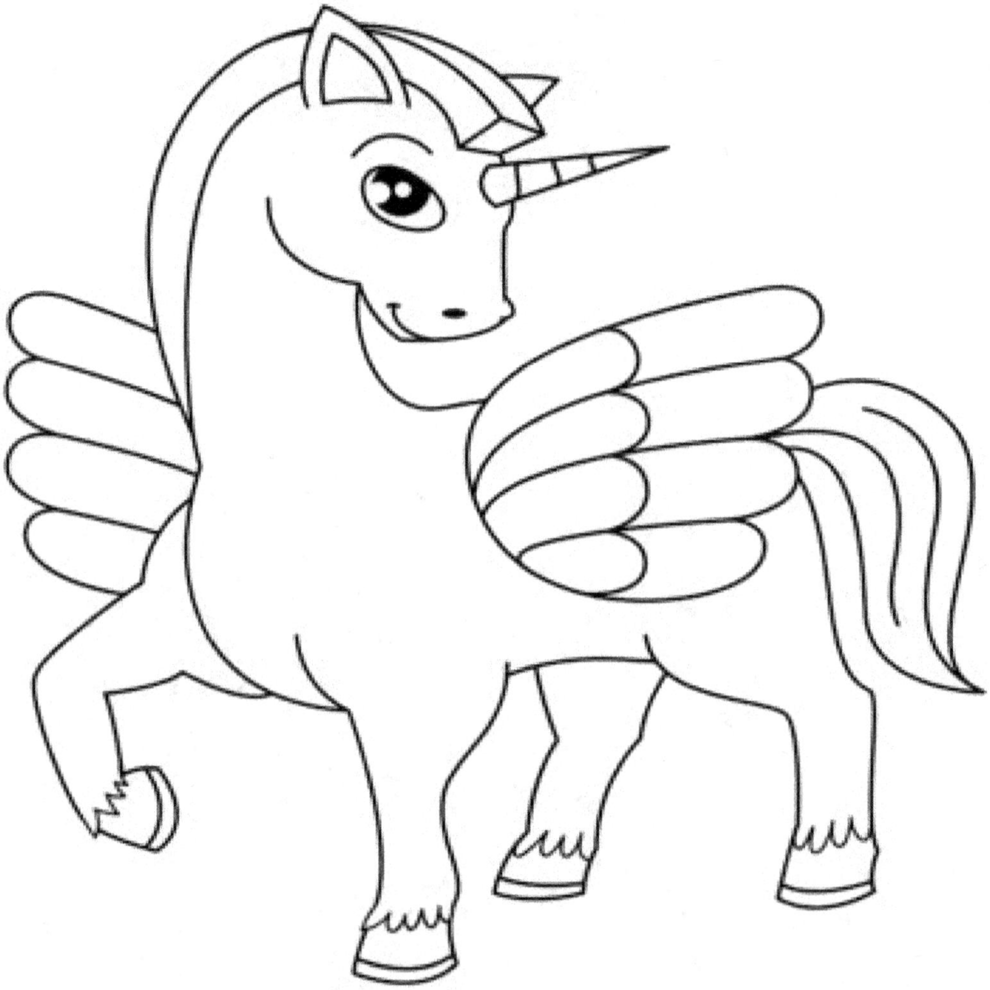

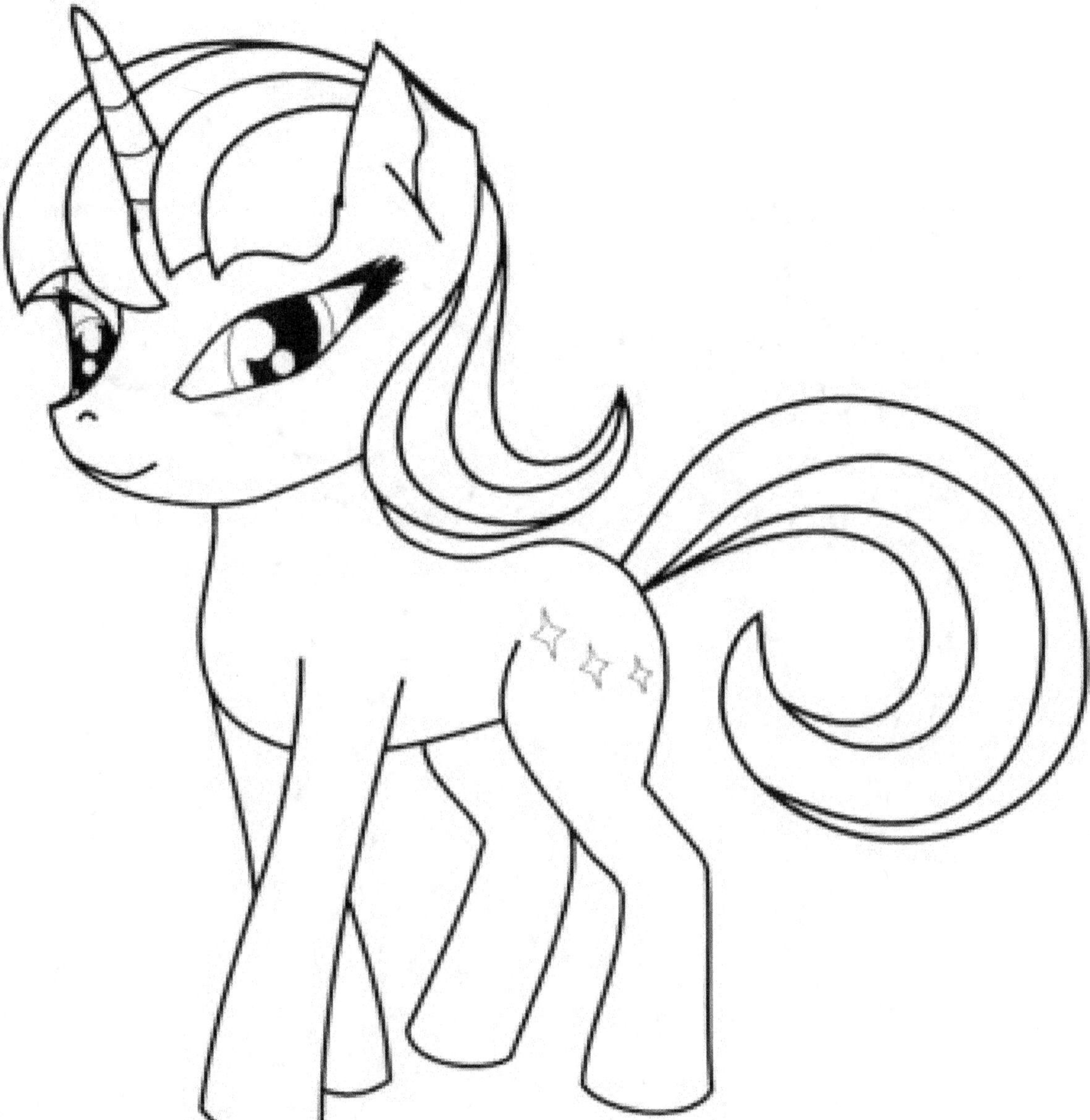

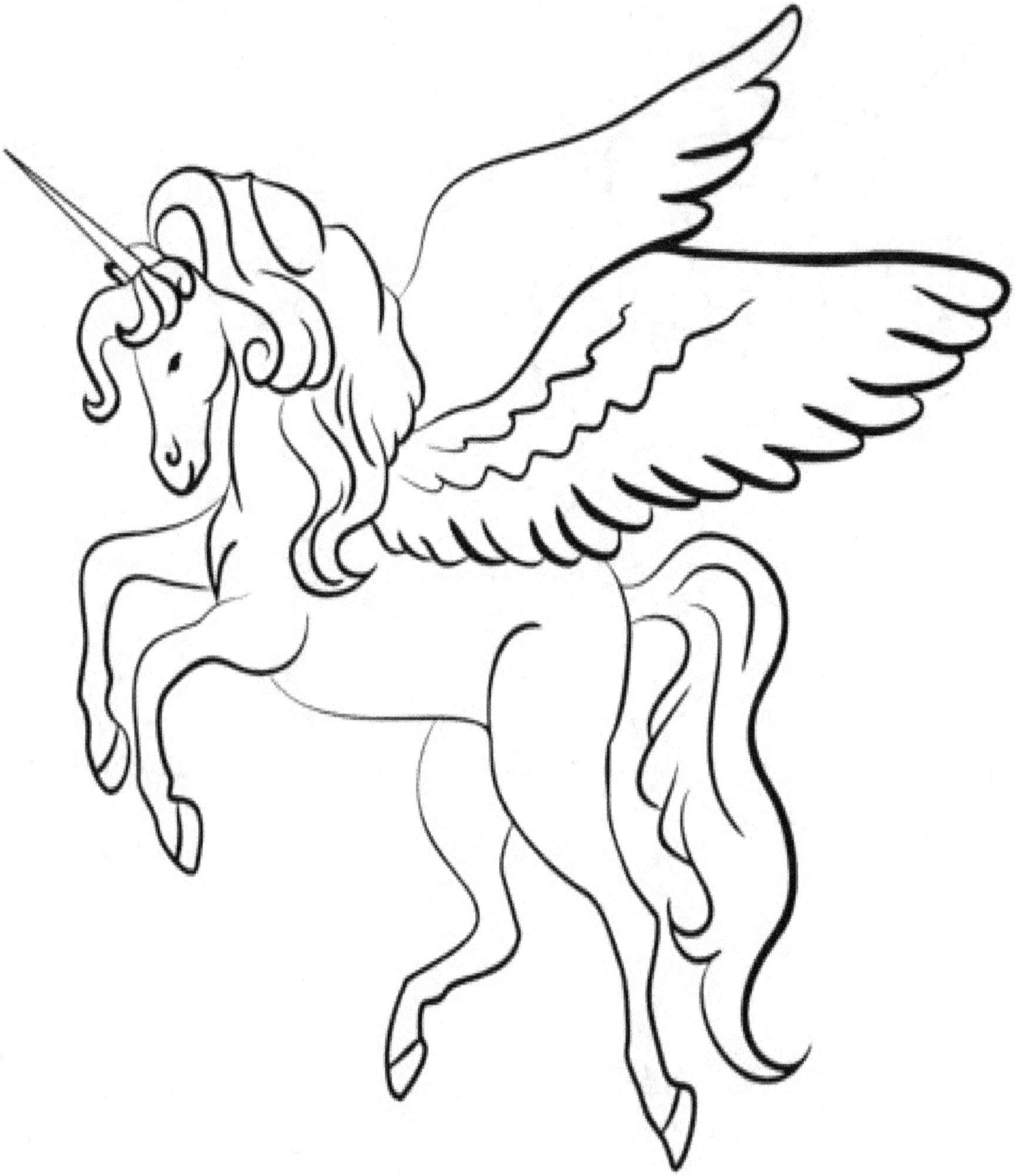

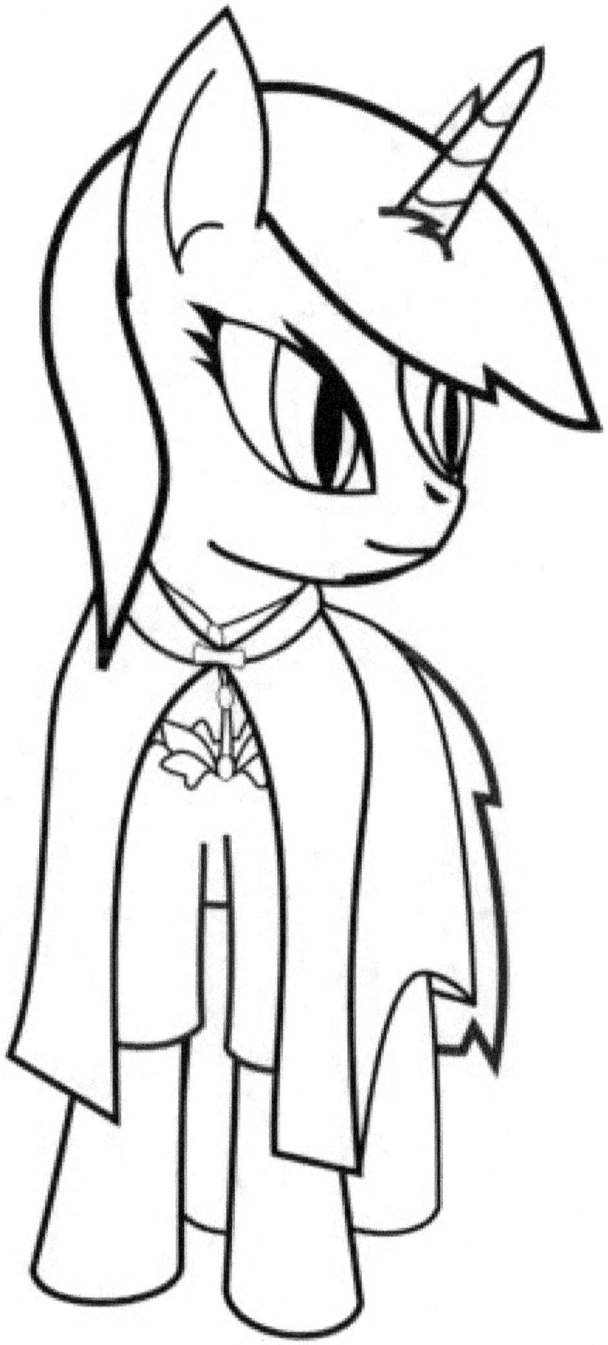

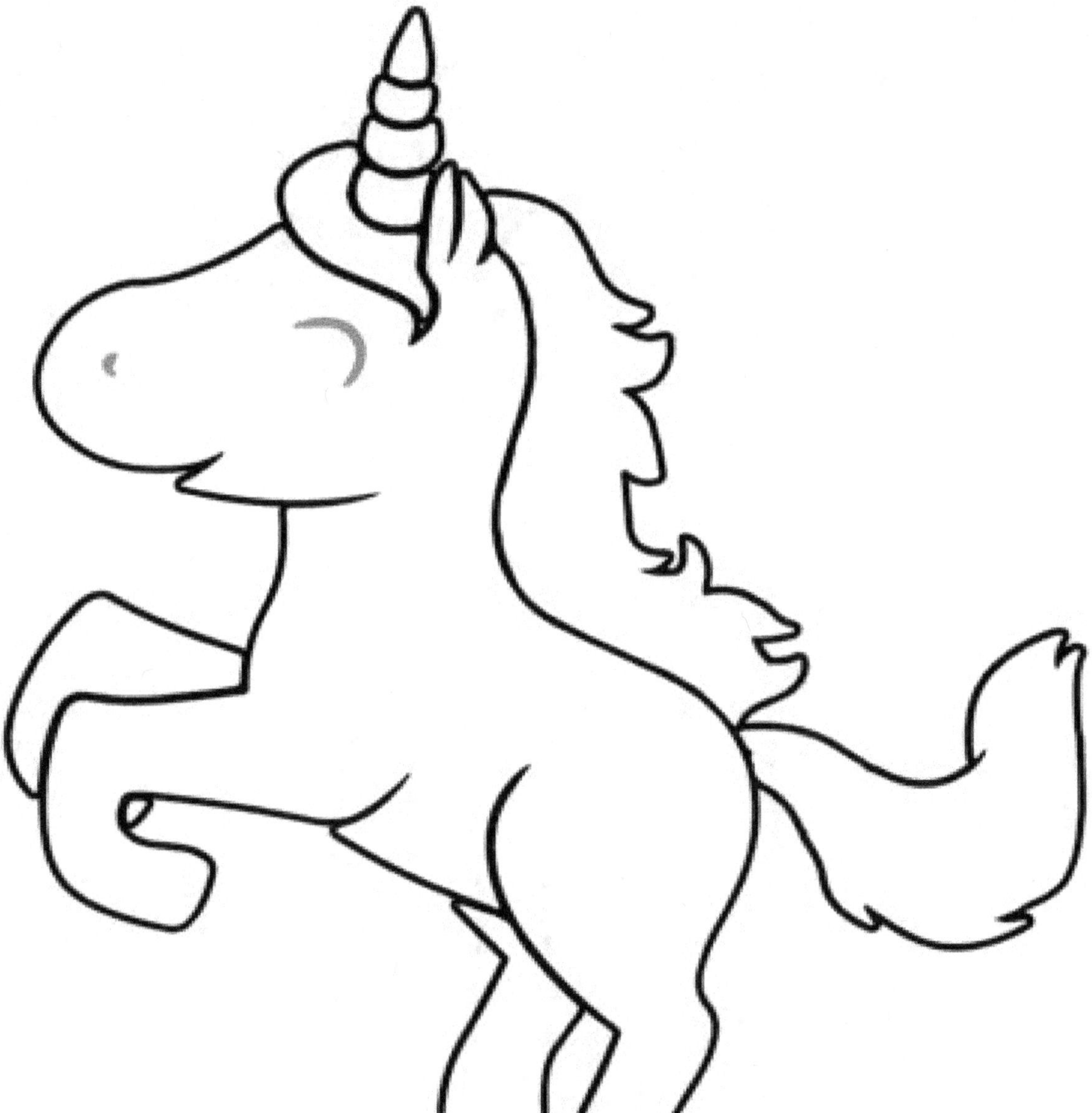

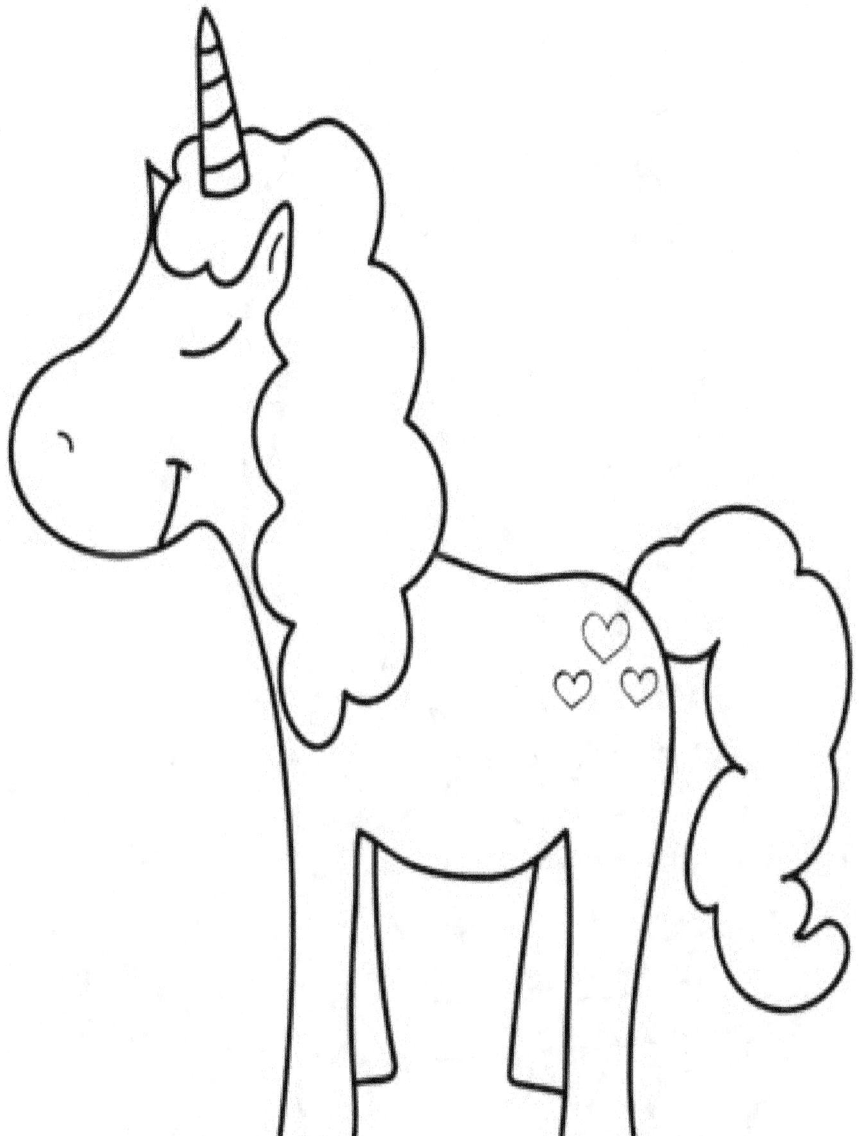

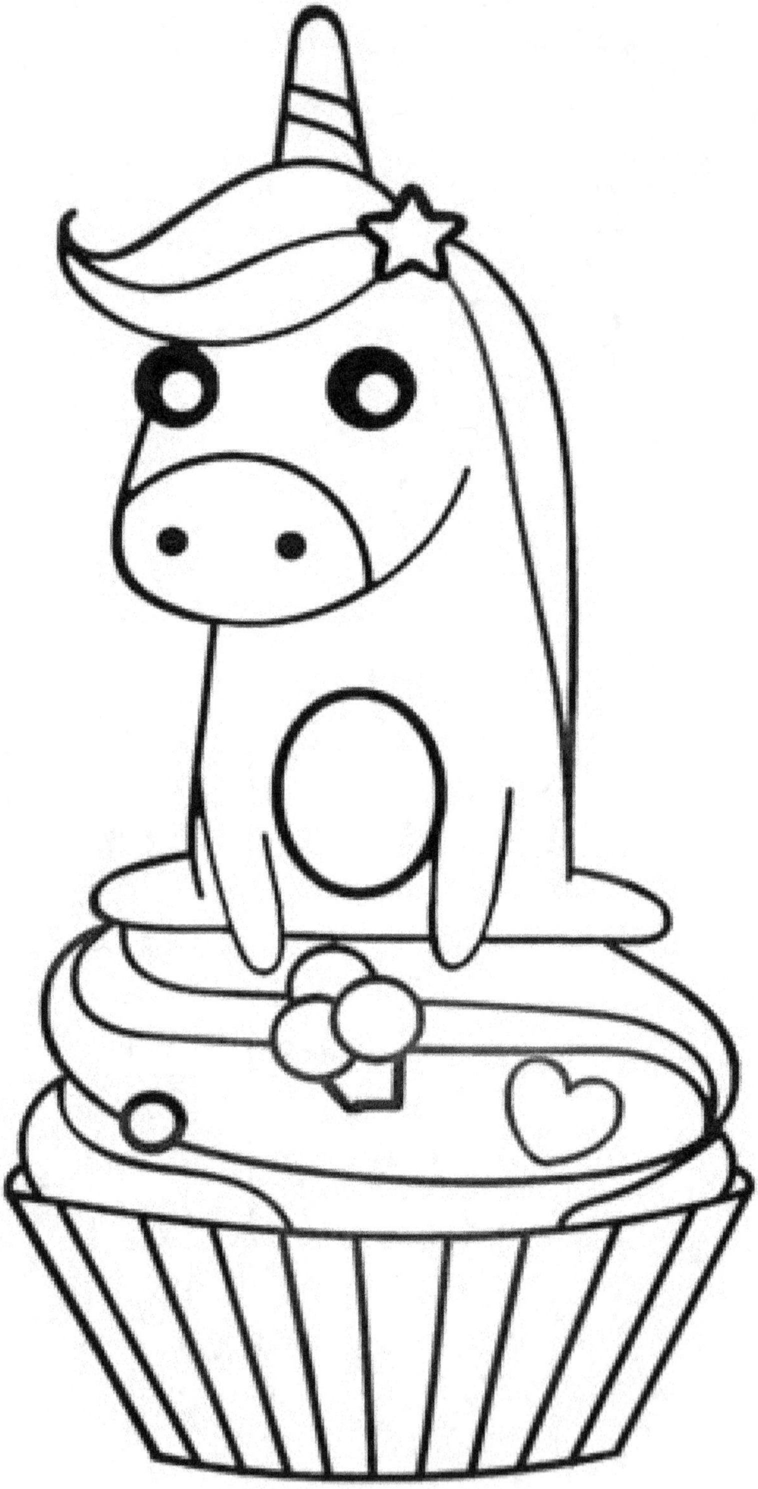

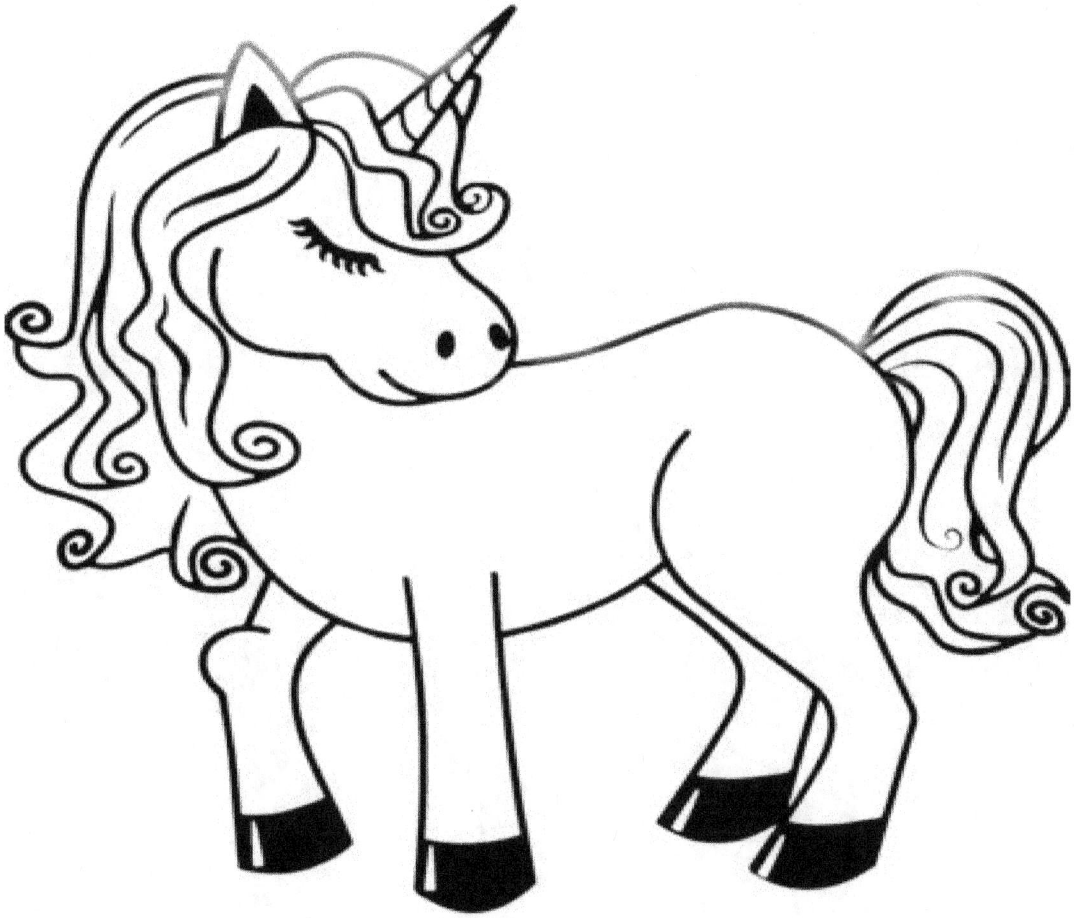

www.ingramcontent.com/pod-product-compliance
Lightning Source LLC
Chambersburg PA
CBHW052043280526
45791CB00010B/3067
* 9 7 8 1 0 7 3 4 5 7 3 3 5 *